Douglas,
the Traveling Dog

Written by Mary Goral
Illustrated by Samantha Goral Maloney

Balboa Press books may be ordered through booksellers or by contacting:

Balboa Press
A Division of Hay House
1663 Liberty Drive
Bloomington, IN 47403
www.balboapress.com
1 (877) 407-4847

ISBN: 978-1-9822-4005-9 (sc)
ISBN: 978-1-9822-4015-8 (e)

Library of Congress Control Number: 2019920836

Print information available on the last page.

Balboa Press rev. date: 12/30/2019

Douglas, the Traveling Dog

Introducing Douglas!

Book 1: The Gifts

A long time ago, when Gram and Grandpa were young–before Grandpa became a lawyer and Gram became a professor–Grandpa brought home a surprise. This surprise fit in his coat pocket and was small, white, and furry.

"What in the world?" asked Gram. "Why, he's no bigger than a guinea pig!"

"I know," replied Grandpa proudly. "I found him alongside the railroad tracks. He was crying and whining–probably abandoned by someone."

"He's adorable," said Gram. "What should we name him?"

"He looks like a slug," Grandpa explained. "Let's name him Doug the Slug."

The name stuck but was later lengthened to Douglas.

And just like that, Douglas became a member of the family.

Douglas was a smart and cute puppy. He was mostly white with a brown spot over one eye, one brown ear, and a brown patch at the beginning of his tail. Like most puppies, Douglas grew quickly. His little slug body morphed into a sleek, slender frame accentuated by *very* long legs. He was quite a handsome dog.

As Douglas grew, he began to explore the neighborhood. Back in those days, dogs weren't kept in pens or in fenced-in yards as much as they are today (at least our dogs weren't), and so Douglas had the freedom to check out the streets where he lived. Some days, he'd be gone for long stretches, and Gram and Grandpa would worry about him. But he always came back–some would say like a bad penny!

One day, after he'd been out on one of his long expeditions, Gram noticed something on the front porch that hadn't been there before. Lo and behold, it was a *really* nice welcome mat. It was placed right in front of the door. Maybe it was not quite symmetrical, but it had definitely been placed.

The mat was made of a thick straw-like material and had the word *welcome* written on it in bold black letters. It was a fine mat. Gram couldn't be positive, but she thought Douglas had brought this wonderful gift for her and Grandpa.

A few days after the arrival of the welcome mat, Gram noticed something else new on the front porch. It was a large hunk of cheese!

Gram picked it up, and aside from a few teeth marks and a little drool, it was in perfect shape. And because Gram and Grandpa didn't have much money then, she took it into the kitchen, poured boiling water on it, and served it as part of their dinner that night.

The final gift was probably a more selfish acquisition. Douglas had somehow managed to find a pup tent, which he delivered once again to the front porch!

It was orange and just the right size for him. Gram and Grandpa set it up in the backyard. Douglas spent many a fine, sunny afternoon lounging in his very own personal hideaway.

You may think that this is made up, but every part of this story is true—honestly.

About the Author

Mary Barr Goral, Ph.D., began her career in education over 30 years ago. After teaching in the public schools in Bloomington, IN for 11 years, she received both her masters and doctorate in curriculum studies and math education from Indiana University. Dr. Goral taught in higher education for 12 years and works with Public Waldorf schools, coaching and training teachers through her educational organization, Transformational Teaching.

Dr. Goral originally published books and articles for her academic career. Author or the book "Transformational Teaching: Waldorf-inspired

Methods in the Public School", and over 10 peer-reviewed articles, Dr. Goral has turned her love for writing, children, and dogs into her first children's book. Mother of five and grandmother of eight, Dr. Goral's story of "Douglas the Traveling Dog" is based on the real-life adventures of her dog, Douglas.

Samantha Goral Maloney is a native of Milwaukee, though she has traveled and lived throughout the Midwest. Samantha first fell in love with the fine arts when she was a student at a Waldorf school and later a fine arts high school. She attended Indiana University – Bloomington for her undergraduate degree where she studied Art History. As she entered graduate school at the University of Wisconsin – Milwaukee, she anticipated studying Medieval illuminated manuscripts, but switched gears to focus on museum studies with an emphasis on exhibition displays and visitor experiences. Samantha graduated in 2019 from the University of Wisconsin – Milwaukee Department of Art History with a Master of Arts degree. Her water color paintings in the first of the Douglas books bring even more life and beauty to the pages.

Printed in the United States
By Bookmasters